Earth's GROSSEST Animals

Body Bugs

Alix Wood

WINDMILL BOOKS

New York

Published in 2014 by Windmill Books, An Imprint of Rosen Publishing
29 East 21st Street, New York, NY 10010

Copyright © 2014 Alix Wood Books

Editor: Sara Howell
Designer: Alix Wood

Photo Credits: Cover, 1, 3, 6, 7, 8, 17 top, 20, 21 right, 22, 23, 24, 29 © Shutterstock; 4 left, 16 ©
image source IS2/Fotolia, 4 right © Cosmin Manci/Fotolia, 5 © Rocky Mountain Laboratories,
NIAID; 9 © Astendal/Fotolia, 10 © Piotr Naskrecki, CDC/ Harvard University; 11 © Janice
Harney Carr, Center for Disease Control; 12 and 13 © Juan Gärtner/Fotolia, 14 © Guido Vrola/
Fotolia, 15 top © Jan Andersen/Fotolia, 15 bottom © James Heilman, MD; 17 © Michael
Brunck, NW Lens; 18 © Miramiski/Fotolia, 19 © Goodluz/Fotolia, 21 left © CDC; 25 left ©
Kalumemt; 25 right © Pali A/Fotolia, 26 © Sergey Goruppa/Fotolia, 27 © Wong Sze Fei/Fotolia;
28 © Public Health Library

Library of Congress Cataloging-in-Publication Data

Wood, Alix.
 Body bugs / by Alix Wood.
     pages cm. — (Earth's grossest animals)
 Includes index.
 ISBN 978-1-61533-732-3 (library binding) — ISBN 978-1-61533-781-1 (pbk.) —
 ISBN 978-1-61533-782-8 (6-pack)
 1. Parasitic insects—Juvenile literature. 2. Insects as carriers of disease—Juvenile literature.
 3. Human body—Juvenile literature. I. Title.
 QL496.12.W66 2014
 362.1969'6—dc23
                          2012043714

Manufactured in the United States of America

CPSIA Compliance Information: Batch #BS13WM: For Further Information contact: Windmill Books, New York, New York at 1-866-478-0556

Contents

Make Yourself at Home!

Everything has to live somewhere, but did you know that many living things have made themselves right at home on you?

We hate them, but they love us! Our bodies can make a great home for all kinds of nasty creatures. A living thing that lives in or on another living thing is called a **parasite**. You can pick up parasites in lots of different ways, such as insect bites, walking barefoot, and touching things. You can get them from other people or animals, from water, or by eating raw fruits and vegetables or undercooked meat and fish.

a life-size flea

Many parasites will live on you without you even noticing. It makes sense not to bother us too much. Once we realize they are there, we usually try to get rid of them! Some body bugs are big enough to see, like a flea. Others are so tiny that you need a **microscope** to see them.

Tapeworms grow inside humans. Some tapeworms have been known to grow to over 30 feet (10 m) long! Yuck!

This close-up image of salmonella **bacteria**, colored red, was taken with a scanning electron microscope. It can take images of really tiny stuff we can't see just using our eyes. Salmonella bacteria causes food poisoning.

Horrible Horseflies

Watch out for these bloodsucking monster horseflies. Some can be over 1 inch (2.5 cm) long!

Horseflies give one of the fiercest bites of any fly. Male horseflies just eat **pollen**. It's the females that feed on your blood. They have scissorlike mouthparts that tear at the flesh.

Horsefly young, called **larvae**, look like maggots. Larvae have sharp mouthparts for chewing, too.

Horsefly larvae eat insects, snails, and earthworms. They will happily eat each other as well! Nice.

A horsefly bite is so painful because the fly's mouthparts are like tiny saw blades. The female saws a hole in your skin to soak up the blood. Luckily for us, adult horseflies only live for a few days.

Left uncontrolled, 20-30 horseflies can drain about .4 pints (190 ml) of blood from their victims in as little as 6 hours!

razor-sharp mouthparts

Ticks Stuck in Your Skin

Ticks have eight legs and are more closely related to spiders than insects. You can pick up ticks from walking in long grass with bare skin. They will hitch a ride and make a meal of your blood!

Once they have jumped on, ticks will attach themselves to you by burying their heads into your skin. Ticks have sharp mouthparts rather like tiny crab claws. First they ooze a numbing chemical so their **host** doesn't feel their hard, stabbing mandibles pierce the skin. The mouthparts are barbed so once they are attached, you can't brush them off.

A tick attaches itself to its host by pushing its sharp mandibles into the skin.

A hungry tick is small and flat, like a freckle. Once it starts to feed, its elastic **abdomen** expands to store blood. A female tick can suck up a hundred times its own body weight in blood. Ticks dribble **saliva** into the wound to make the blood flow easily.

Ticks can detect a passing animal or human by its breath and body heat.

This is a close-up image of a tick's head and mouthparts. Ticks' saliva contains bacteria and can spread diseases.

barbed mouthparts

Don't Let the Bedbugs Bite

Just as you are settling down to sleep, a tiny, hungry little bug may be waking up in your own bedroom. And guess who's on the menu?

Bedbugs live in and around mattresses. They pop up and feed on you when you are asleep. They are so tiny they can hide anywhere in and around the bedroom. Bedbugs can hitch a ride in clothes, luggage, or just about anything that a small appleseed-sized insect can get into. They are pretty hard to kill, and they can go over a year without food.

Bedbugs find you in the night from your body's warmth and by sensing the carbon dioxide that you breathe out.

A female bedbug can lay over 500 eggs in her lifetime. Once the eggs hatch the bedbugs will immediately begin to feed. After five weeks they become mature adults capable of breeding, too.

Bedbugs have been known to walk as far as 100 feet (30.5 m) in order to feed on their host.

Bedbugs pierce the skin of their host with long, sharp mouthparts, colored purple in this close-up image (right). The tips of the mouthparts have small teeth which move backward and forward to cut a path through the skin. In the center is a food tube and a smaller tube for saliva, both colored red. When bedbugs have finished feeding, they pull up their mandibles and fold them back under their heads!

Mighty Mites

Dust mites are tiny bugs that love eating your dead skin cells. You can only see them with a microscope. They don't bite you, but they can make you ill.

Dust mites love to live anywhere where they can feast on flakes of old skin. They love mattresses and pillows. A typical used mattress may have anywhere from 100,000 to 10 million mites inside. Mites like to be warm and moist, so they love the inside of a mattress when someone is on it. Humans shed about 0.2 ounce (5.6 g) of dead skin each week.

Through a microscope you can see a dust mite's eight hairy legs. They have no eyes or antennae. Their head area is just made up of mouthparts!

dust mites eating

So maybe eating up all our old, dead skin is a good thing? The problem with dust mites is their droppings, which cause **asthma** and **allergies**. About 10 percent of people are allergic to dust mites.

Ten percent of the weight of a two-year-old pillow is actually dead mites and their droppings. That's gross!

Germs and Body Fungus

Germs can grow on us and sometimes make us ill. **Viruses**, bacteria, and **fungi** can all live on our bodies.

Bacteria are so small you need to use a powerful microscope to see them. We only know we are being attacked by them when we get symptoms, like a sore throat or an ear infection.

a magnified image of rod-shaped bacteria

Bacteria are so small it takes a million of them to cover a pinhead. No wonder they can hide so well!

Fungi are like plants, but they cannot make their own food from soil, water, and air like plants can. Instead, fungi get their food from plants, people, and animals. They love to live in damp, warm places, like between your toes! Athlete's foot is caused by a fungus. It makes the skin flake and itch. The fungi spread from shower floors, wet towels, and footwear.

The scales and cracked skin seen here are caused by the foot fungus called athlete's foot.

Itchy Fleas

Fleas eat 15 times their own weight in food a day! And that food is blood! Cat fleas, which actually live on both cats and dogs, love biting humans, so make sure you check your pet's fur and bed regularly.

Fleas' bodies are tall and flat so they can move easily between the fur on their host. Being flat also helps them avoid being crushed. Fleas are small, wingless insects. Most have bristles and spines, particularly on their legs, that help the flea to hold on to the fur, hair, or feathers of its host. These bristles stop the fleas from falling off during grooming or preening.

comblike bristles

Rat fleas are thought to have caused the bubonic plague back in the 1300s. In just two years, 25 million people died of the plague! The flea caught the disease from the rat and spread it by biting humans.

A flea can jump over 150 times its own size. If a man had the same strength, he could jump over 900 feet (275 m) high. That's as high as a skyscraper. A flea can jump 30,000 times without taking a break, too. High-speed photographs of fleas jumping show that they can do somersaults in the air and even land on their hosts upside down!

Some entertainers make flea circuses (left) to show off their skills! They don't really use fleas, though. It's just pretend.

FLEA CIRCUS

Nasty Nits and Head Lice

Head lice are very small but you'll know if you catch them. Your head will itch and itch. A female head louse lays around 90 eggs in her lifetime. The eggs are called nits.

Head lice are parasites that feed on human blood. They can't jump or fly. They travel from one head to another by crawling. They are good crawlers and can move easily from head to head when people are close together. Head lice can't survive more than 48 hours off a host head. Sometimes they hide in hats or bedding, but they will not live for long unless an unwary head passes close by and they crawl on board.

This is a magnified image of some head lice. They are really only the size of a pinhead.

Lice eggs, or nits, look like tiny yellow or brown dots before they hatch. After hatching, the remaining shell looks white or clear. The best way to get rid of head lice and nits is with a special comb with very close-together teeth. Daily combing will help dislodge any that may have crawled onto you during the day. The quicker you get rid of them, the less likely they can lay eggs in your hair.

This girl is having her hair checked for head lice with a fine-tooth comb.

Head lice have been around for millions of years. Dried up lice and their eggs have been found on the hair of Egyptian mummies!

Tapeworm Attack!

Tapeworms almost seem to know that the best place to hide on the human body is inside it! They live inside human **intestines,** and they love it there.

Tapeworms get into your body if you eat or drink something infected with a worm or its eggs. You can get tapeworms from undercooked meat, infected soil, or animal waste. Once inside the body, the tapeworm head attaches to the inner wall of the intestines using tiny hooks and suckers. The tapeworm then feeds off the food that you eat.

Tapeworms can live inside a person's intestines for up to 25 years!

Always wash your hands after playing outside. Tapeworm eggs can lurk in the soil.

Tapeworms are made up of **segments**. Tapeworms get longer by growing new segments at their head end. Old segments will break off the tail end of the tapeworm and come out of your body in your waste. Tapeworm segments can live for months in the environment, waiting for a new host to come.

Some tapeworms grow to more than a thousand segments long.

hooks

suckers

a long tapeworm

tapeworm's head

Malaria and Mosquitoes

Mosquitoes' high-pitched buzz is a really annoying noise, and their bite can be itchy, too. In some countries, mosquitoes aren't just a nuisance, though. They are also deadly.

Mosquitoes can spread a disease called **malaria**. Mosquitoes pass the disease on when they bite. The malaria parasites enter the victim's bloodstream and then invade their blood and liver.

Mosquito bites can get very red, swollen, and itchy.

Over one million people die from malaria each year. Mosquitoes also spread other diseases by passing infected blood from one host to another.

It's the female mosquito that bites. Mosquitoes feed on nectar from flowers and fruits, but the female also needs the proteins from blood to reproduce.

This mosquito is piercing the skin with its proboscis. Its body is full of blood.

Female mosquitoes lay up to fifty eggs at a time. With enough of your blood for their lunch they can lay eggs every three days! The eggs hatch into larvae in 48 hours. After a few weeks they will turn into adult mosquitoes.

Mosquitoes bite using a **proboscis**, which is like a long, sharp nose. They inject a special chemical with their saliva to stop the blood from clotting, so they get a free-flowing meal. Usually the host has no idea he has been bitten until it is too late and the itchy bump appears.

Really Disgusting Flies

Even the common housefly can be really gross. They have some pretty disgusting habits. The botfly is even worse and could just give you nightmares. You have been warned!

Houseflies vomit on the food they land on, puking up digestive juices and saliva. This helps break the food down to a soup they can suck through their straw-like tongue. Houseflies also lay their eggs in dead flesh, which hatch out into crawly maggots.

Houseflies love to eat human and animal waste. Then they carry the germs from the waste on their feet and mouthparts. When they land on us or on our food they can spread disease.

Botfly larvae burrow inside the bodies of mammals—even humans! Botflies lay their eggs on mosquitoes. When the mosquito bites a person, eggs fall onto the host and hatch. The botfly larva will then chew its way into the host's body. There it eats away at the host's flesh for 5-6 weeks until it bursts its way out of the hole it has eaten in the host's skin. The maggot becomes an adult botfly in about 20 days, and the cycle begins again.

The hole that a botfly larva makes in the host's flesh acts as a breathing tube. Every few minutes the larva will pop its head up from the hole to breathe!

Botflies are also called gadflies.

This is a life-size botfly larva. Only remove a larva with professional help as they can burst, causing serious infection.

Bloodsucking Leeches

Leeches are bloodsuckers that lurk in water or damp places. They have powerful suckers which grip onto their hosts while they feed on their blood.

A few types of leech suck human blood. Some have toothlike blades that leave a Y-shaped mark on their host's skin. Others suck blood through a proboscis which acts like a straw. A leech can suck up to ten times its weight in blood in about 30 minutes. When it's full, it drops off the host.

Leeches mainly prey on people playing in ponds and lakes. They sense ripples in the water and then swim over for a meal.

Leeches have suckers at both ends which attach to your skin. The sucker on the left has the mouthparts.

Some leeches can bite through a hippo's tough skin, while others live on the gums of the Nile crocodile. Some big species may get to be more than 10 inches (25 cm) long.

Like many bloodsuckers, leeches' saliva has a special substance that keeps blood flowing and stops it from clotting. Leeches are so good at this that doctors have started using the chemical they make to help stop blood clots. Leeches have been used in medicine as far back as 2,500 years ago, when they were used for bloodletting in ancient India.

When a leech is feeding on its host, its saliva makes the blood very watery.

Face Invaders

Some bugs make themselves at home on your face. Eyelash mites live in the tiny openings called **follicles** where eyelash hair grows out of. Bacteria are very happy living on your tongue, too!

The picture on the right is of an eyelash mite. Mites are almost see-through, with eight short legs. Their bodies are covered with scales which help them cling to the hair follicle.

eyelash mite

If you have a microscope, try gently removing an eyelash or eyebrow hair and look for mites. Adults are more likely to have eyelash mites than children.

Mites don't like the light, but at night they might take a walk around your face, at a speed of 3 to 6 inches (8–15 cm) per hour! Eyelash mites live, reproduce, and die inside your hair follicles.

Do you brush your tongue? It's a good idea to, so you can get rid of unwanted bacteria that hide there.

There are about 40,000 bacteria living in a person's mouth. Bacteria feed on leftovers and dead cells. They love the wet and warm surroundings.

Bacteria hide in all the tiny grooves between the taste buds on the surface of your tongue. They are covered by a blanket of mucus. Some bacteria cause bad breath.

A lot of the bacteria that live on your tongue are good for you. Bacteria help break down food you eat, and eat up old body cells. They can also fight other germs and help protect us from infection.

Glossary

abdomen (AB-duh-mun)
The body cavity containing the chief digestive organs.

allergies (A-lur-jeez)
Abnormal reactions to substances, often causing sneezing, itching, or rashes.

asthma (AZ-muh)
Difficulty breathing and a tightness in the chest.

bacteria (bak-TIR-ee-uh)
Single-celled microorganisms that can cause disease.

follicles (FO-lih-kelz)
Small cavities in the skin from which hairs grow.

fungi (FUN-jy)
Plantlike living things that do not have leaves, flowers, or green color and that do not make their own food.

host (HOHST)
A living animal or plant on or in which a parasite lives.

intestines (in-TES-tinz)
Long tubes in the body that help digest food, absorb nutrients, and carry waste matter to be discharged.

larvae (LAHR-vee)
Young wingless forms that hatch from eggs of many insects.

malaria (muh-LER-ee-uh)
A disease passed by the bite of mosquitoes.

microscope
(MY-kruh-skohp)
An instrument that makes magnified images.

parasite (PER-uh-syt)
A living thing which lives in or on another living thing.

pollen (PAH-lin)
Tiny particles in flowers that fertilize the seeds.

proboscis (pruh-BAH-sus)
A long tube-shaped organ in the mouth region of an invertebrate.

saliva (suh-LY-vuh)
A fluid in the mouth that helps with digestion.

segments (SEG-ments)
Parts into which a thing is divided or naturally separates.

viruses (VY-rus-es)
Something tiny that causes a disease.

WEBSITES
For web resources related to the subject of this book, go to:
www.windmillbooks.com/weblinks
and select this book's title.

Read More

Fleisher, Paul. *Parasites: Latching on to a Free Lunch*. Discovery! Minneapolis, MN: Twenty-First Century Books, 2006.

Silverstein, Alvin, and Virginia Silverstein. *Tapeworms, Foot Fungus, Lice, and More: The Yucky Disease Book*. Yucky Science. Berkeley Heights, NJ: Enslow Publishers, 2011.

Somervill, Barbara. *Mosquitoes: Hungry for Blood*. Bloodsuckers. New York: PowerKids Press, 2008.

Index